Life Isn't What It Seems

Poetry That's Based On A True Story

LAVELL HARRIS

ARPress

ARPress
45 Dan Road Suite 36
Canton MA 02021

Hotline: 1(800) 220-7660
Fax: 1(855) 752-6001

Ordering Information:
Quantity sales. Special discounts are available on quantity purchases by corporations, associations, and others. For details, contact the publisher at the address above.

Printed in the United States of America.

ISBN-13:   Paperback   979-8-89389-633-6
              eBook   979-8-89389-634-3

Library of Congress Control Number: 2024921303

ACKNOWLEDGMENTS

FIRST, I WANT TO GIVE ALL PRAISE TO MY LORD AND SAVIOR JESUS CHRIST FOR GIVING ME THE STRENGTH AND MOTIVATION TO WRITE THIS BOOK. LIFE ISN'T WHAT IT SEEMS IS A POETRY BOOK THAT TALKS ON SOME OF THE HARDSHIPS THAT I PERSONALLY EXPERIENCED WHILE COMMITTING MYSELF TO CHRIST. I WOULD LOVE TO THANK MY FAMILY FOR SUPPORTING EVERYTHING I EVER WANTED TO DO IN LIFE AND CONTINUOUSLY PROGRESSING TO MAKE THINGS HAPPEN FOR MYSELF AND OTHERS. YET, MOST OF ALL I WANT TO THANK MY FAMILY FOR PRAYING FOR ME WHEN I DID NOT WANT TO PRAY FOR MYSELF. TO MY BUSINESS PARTNERS AND INVESTORS, I TRULY THANK YOU ALL FOR PUTTING UP WITH ME, AND CONTINUOUSLY WORKING WITH ME NO MATTER WHAT. I PERSONALLY WANT TO THANK ALL MY SPIRITUAL BROTHERS AND SISTERS IN CHRIST, BOTH KNOWN AND UNKNOWN, FOR ALL YOUR PRAYERS HAVE HELPED ME THROUGH SO MUCH. TWO ALL OF MY MENTORS, TEACHERS, COACHES, FRIENDS, AND ASSOCIATES I THANK JESUS CHRIST FOR PLACING YOU ALL IN MY LIFE TO TEACH ME THINGS THAT I WILL ALWAYS VALUE. I KNOW THAT I AM STANDING ON THE SHOULDERS OF THE ONES THAT CAME BEFORE ME, AND I KNOW IT IS NOT GOING TO BE EASY TO FILL THEIR SHOES OR EVEN MATCH UP TO THEIR WORK. I TRULY THANK JESUS CHRIST FOR THE ONES WHO PAVED THE WAY FOR PEOPLE LIKE

ME AND STARTING A LEGACY THAT WILL LIVE ON FOREVER. MOST OF ALL I WANT TO THANK MYSELF FOR FIRST TAKING THE NECESSARY STEPS TO BE A BORN-AGAIN CHRISTIAN AND HUMAN BEING. YES, I WAS BORN INTO CHRISTIANITY BUT ALSO MADE SO MANY MISTAKES TOO. WRITING THIS BOOK HONESTLY CHANGED MY LIFE. I NEVER THOUGHT I WOULD BE ABLE TO TELL MY STORY SO EARLY IN MY WRITING CAREER, BUT CHRIST ONCE ALLOWED ME TO LEARN THAT MY TESTIMONY COULD BE SOMEONE ELSE'S BREAKTHROUGH.

WORDS FROM THE AUTHOR

I DECREE AND DECLARE BLESSINGS UPON YOU, WE SOMETIMES FALL SHORT OF GOD'S MERCY AND GRACE, BUT I REBUKE EVERY TEMPTATION, EVERY HARDSHIP, EVERY BACKSLIDING DECISION IN THE NAME OF JESUS. I PRAY HEALING AND DELIVERANCE OVER YOUR FAMILY AND HOUSEHOLD RIGHT NOW IN THE NAME OF JESUS. FOR I PRAY A BREAKTHROUGH AND NEW BEGINNING WILL COME YOUR WAY AND YOU GET TO KNOW JESUS CHRIST FOR YOURSELF OR BUILD A CLOSER RELATIONSHIP WITH HIM. I PRAY THAT YOU LIVE LIFE WITH NO REGRETS. FOR WHAT GOD HAS IN STORAGE FOR YOU, LET NO MAN DESTROY. I PRAY PEACE AND JOY UPON YOU, AND WITH JESUS CHRIST PERMISSION I PRAY THAT YOU NOT ONLY READ MY STORY BUT ALLOW IT TO BE A BLESSING UNTO YOU, AS IT HAS FOR ME, AND I PRAY THIS AND SO MUCH MORE IN JESUS NAME, AMEN.

CONTENTS

LIFE

Appreciated (Part 2)

Because of you I am here
I'm alive and well
I am who I am because of you
From the love that's given
To the tears that were shared
The laughter from you
Fights of the undeserving
Because of you I am here
I'm living to learn
Also, learning to live, because of you
Because of you
Because of you
I am the man that I am, because of you
All of you
Related or not
Supportive or not
I appreciate you
I appreciate you
I appreciate you
You, and you too
All of you
Words cannot explain
Actions will never be enough
You all are greatly appreciated
Thanks

Cherish

Water splashing

I hear the sirens

Rushing footsteps as the people howling

The sun was shining

Seems to be cool now

Daily activities with constant frowns

Pigeons flying

Not enough space on the ground

What use to be enjoyable summer times?

There are funeral services scheduled for each day now

The young replaced the old

The heart of others match the icicles in the cold

Love can't be found anymore

Just the reality of unfaithful parents walking out the door

Did you ever have someone care for your child?

Please cherish every moment of your natural life

It's only a phase

Livable moments before it's too late

Cherish every moment of your life

It could be taken away

You could just up and pass away

Gone from a natural death

Only Jesus has the last words

Cherish every moment of your life

Good or bad

Cherish the ones in your life

For it could be that water splashing day

Children used to play

Now bullets greet them

Start flying their way

Wake up and cherish everything in your life

Dreams Do Come True

Who told you that you wasn't going to make it?

I did

I told you that you don't have what it takes

I told you that you weren't known enough

I told you that you don't have the money to do much

I told you that you're not skillful enough

You lack talent

I told you to give up

I told you that dreaming is not for you

I told you

I told you and you listened

You are me

I am you

So yes

I let myself down

I was my own roadblock

I was the main one not believing

I couldn't see it

Now look at me

I am living

I am a success

Hard to understand

I am a professional

If that

I made a name
Put the work in
Still progressing
Known to have an income now
Known to have supporters now
I apologize to my own self
Jesus is good to me
look at me now
Dreams do come true

I Know My Time Is Coming

I've paid the cost

Somethings I've lost

Knowing that I could only be the master of my own faith

I've paid the cost

When I misbehaved and disobeyed

The ways I'll say self-destruction regulated

In my brain

Self-worth of an intoxicated soul

that will never be the same

Going without not knowing there's greatness

in the ashes I'm blowing

Petty rude and disrespectful

Closing eyes and covering ears is just so stressful

I know my time is coming

I Needed You

Just when I needed you
You're always there on time
You comfort me
You smile with me just like I knew you would
Just when I needed you
You're always on time
You laugh with me
You make me sing
In ways you didn't know you could
Just when I needed you
You always take care of me
You know my needs
My wants and
greeds
Never knew how much you loved me
Just when I needed you
Things had to end
I said good-bye
This made me cry
Knowing deep inside we're all going to die
Just when I needed you
I tried to call your name
I feel pain
Things are not the same
Me knowing
I needed you

If I Die Young

Before I continue I would like to say I love everyone
If I die young will everything be ok?
Will my family and friends be able to hold on?
Will they weep for my exit from the world?
but smile in my honor, in remembrance?
Before I move forward I'll like to say that I apologize
For anything that I've done
And the words that have been said
If I die young
Not wishing nor hoping upon it but just in case
For the lies I've told and the people I've hurt
To the ones I've let down and the others I just didn't Listen to
If I die young
Will my work be in vain and will my legacy die?
Most of all who'll care and be there looking over me
To speak the words of emotions and truth
If I die young
Will I just be another shirt and button picture?
And all people could say is R.I.P
I feel my life was made for me to be all that I am
And all that I want to be
But living in victory for the reason I am
Who I am is because Christ is within me
If I die young
Would I leave my mark on the world?
Have I left it already?

How will people handle my exit?

And will people realize I'm gone?

Have my time here on Earth been worth the memories?

The love I have for others is even greater than the love I have for myself

There are ways that I've inspired and uplifted the ones that enter and exit my life like it never happened

But it did

Only if I knew what could've been and what people thought about

Me as I lay in my casket

But only if I die young

I'm Not Too Sure

"You have lots of time"

I really don't like when people say that

Not saying it's not true, it's just hard to believe

"You have lots of time"

Only if people could see that people are dying every day

People around my age and younger losing their lives

So please don't say "you have lots of time"

When you starting to like girls and really thinking about boys now

Don't take away a teenager's fun

Teach them the right and wrong ways

"You have lots of time"

To think about sex as the older ones may say

Crazy how some lost their virginity in between elementary and the first week of high school

Congrats to the ones still waiting on the right one

"You have lots of time"

Children interacting in games that turns into sexual activities

Crazy how no one told us then

So please don't say "you have lots of time"

We are afraid

So we're doing us for now

Needless to say, no telling when we'll die

We are afraid

Well I know I am

With all the killing

So many of us are now getting married at young ages

Having kids and getting tattoos

Getting piercings

Living life, doing wrong and doing right

We call it living

Despite what we're going through

"You have lots of time"

Yeah that might and could be true

What's happening today in this day and age?

All we still have to endure

As for me

I'm living life

Because now a days you can't be too sure

It feels Like I Hit Rock Bottom

So many advices

Which way to go?

How to succeed in life when all you hear is no?

There's barely positive leaders and role models

as I develop and grow

I didn't listen as much

So it feels like I hit rock bottom faster than you said so

Just Passing Through

They ask me to be sincere

Show my real emotions and don't hide my tears

As I use to hear the voices of love ones and friends

That's now disappeared

Souls of the deceased circling around me

Trying to hear me speak

Shaking the spirits off me

Too much cold

It feels like Death is looking for me

I stand naked

Looking from my head to my feet wondering why we keep trying to improve

Only to hear ashes to ashes and dust to dust

Our souls have been freed while our organs being auctioning off

This is not a sad poem to mourn and carry on

I used to speak with the elders

as they held me and helped me get through

Crying yet smiling

each time it's that time to view another body

Hoping my family and I can get through the service

as we view

Crying those sad yet rejoicing tears

As they are just passing through

Now I Understand

All I wanted to do was write
Say a few rhymes and metaphors of poetry
Leading me to becoming published and public
Those mouthpieces start dialing me
Option 1 2 3 and 4,
my pride disconnected by the time I hung up on representative number 5
Dial tone of holding long started to sound like music in my ears
Damn you operator!
Misleading directions of switching over and over to the point somebody
needs Folgers in their cup to get me to the right extension
These mouthpieces of convincing and bribery
Ambition and photography wants me to see the bigger picture
All I wanted to do was write poetry
Pickpocketing me all just to market me
Leading my book to the next level while money disappearing from me
Damn you mouthpieces!
The operator and customer service representative playing with my
intelligence
Option 1 2 and 3
I'll just do us all a favor and oops!
I disconnected
Thanks for calling me

One Love

I'll never apologize for loving you the way I do
Some call it respect
While others would call me a fool
Well I'll say it
I love you
From the top of your head to the soul of your feet
From the ways of your belief
To your personality
From the tone of your skin
To just everything about you
I love you
Yeah I said it
I'm crazy about you
No matter if you're a man or a woman
No matter if you're tall or short
No matter if you're gay or straight
No matter if you're dark or light
I'm crazy about you
I love you
I have one love for you
One love and one love only for everybody

Royal (Part 2)

Here I am
Great and mighty
The king of my damage
The leader of my image and
Here I am
The one that you marked
The one that you departed
The one that you made life hard for
Yet I am here
The boy of many stories
The one you want to hurry
The guy you talked dirty about
But here I am
Here I stand
Hands in my pockets
No shaking hands
It's my demand
You say you know me
But I don't know you
I thought I did
But it was the mask you wore

No coming back now

You played me like a fool

No no no

You're not allowed to speak

I'm not God

But you should be bowing to me

Telling me you're sorry

You should've known better

You should've known that I am royal

Trying To Hold Back Tears

I sit on my bed thinking about you
All our lives
Reading people Facebook posts
Seeing that sad emoji face with tears
It feels weird and so untrue
Just remembering yesterday
Some days ago
I was just around you
I just saw you
Now I'm reading all these RIP's statuses
I've OD from feeling the lowest
Never done drugs but it felt like it was over
I'm hurt
Too many people I know died
It still hurts
Even the ones I don't know
Just to see another body unite with the dirt
That stuff hurts
Trying to hold back these tears
We are all going to die
That don't mean we can't fear
I'm feeling like R-Kelly when he wrote "I Wish"
While Puff Daddy, Faith Evans, and 112 continually sing
"I'll Be Missing You"

Even DRS playing in the background will make a thug cry in that
"Gangsta Lean"
Just knowing you all in a better place
Even though I'm wishing I can turn back the hands of time
Yelling in my mind "my God my God tell them they don't have to fight
no more"
As I'm trying to hold back these tears
Just know I'll be missing you all

Unspoken Words

Maybe I could've said more
Would you all have listened
Life is too short and little kids are missing
Not to mention all the ones that died in these streets
Can barely eat
Fighting everyday just to keep shoes on their feet
Used clothes
Just as good as new to me
I'm tired of struggling
Praying that next bullet is not for me
I should've said more
Now faces that I care about is gone now
Young souls have been taking away now
Most are dead
Others ran away
It's the truth
I'm deeply in shock that I can't see your face again
Not only your face
His face
Her face
Their faces
When will we wake the hell up to notice that we have to do better?
It's sad
Dead or in jail, right?
I can't even close my eyes without thinking about tomorrow night
It's like a flash went off and you ALL in the next life

I just should've said more

This is too much for me right now

Body after body and tears flooding the gates now

I'll be there soon

You all didn't deserve that despite what others say

I watched some of you grow into the men and women

I knew was inside

Trying to turn you all lives around I swear

I was watching the progress

Now some I have to say goodbye to

While others I'm praying for

Praying that you all would make a change

And Lord please forgive me

Quick money

Sex

So call street love is killing

It's killing me

I don't even gang bang but the streets love me

Christ put it in my heart to love everybody

Told me to go back and try to reach somebody

I wish I could've said more

Would you all have listened?

It hurts to know some in jail while others in the ground

Some ran away while others can't be found

I love you all and we'll see each other around

Will I Lose My Dignity?

Will I lose my dignity?

Will someone care?

As I sit in this chair

Thoughts reappear

As I yell to the echoes of one voice

The silent roar

Seeking a stream of light

The stream of life awaits me

Walking through the unknown where society buried me

Humanity lost me

While the economy made me the victim of a strong-arm robbery

Will I awake tomorrow from this nightmare?

My eyes connected with the beam of light

As I wish for a hole or door

What's in store?

Finally feeling like the end until I stepped on that transporter

Blue skies turned to no skies

As Mother Nature has gone missing

Father Time died

Sitting here and I realize

Will I lose my dignity?

Will someone care?

Will I awake tomorrow from this nightmare?

You Don't Even Care

Now that I see your true colors shining out your pores
This will only be the real beginning of your feelings toward me
How could it be that I cared so much?
In return I'm being disrespected
I never wanted to see your colors displayed in this reality
You don't even care
I yelled for help
I walked alone
Seeking for a little attention like an orphan with no home
You don't even care
I thought about praying
Could I just be talking?
Killing my own self
You don't even care
I'm losing my mind
People sometimes not there
How could I be loved when I never cared?
Just my "pen to this paper, right?"
You don't even care

NOTES

NOTES

LOVE AND WAR

Heart To Heart

Heart to heart
Friend to friend
It hurts me to know how fast you found another man
Maybe I wasn't your type
Maybe I didn't stand a chance
You could've just left me in your shadows
It's hard to be your friend
I listened closely
I held your hand
Being the one that you could come to when you were having problems
with your boyfriend
You're right
I don't know him
I never even saw him
Yet the pain that he leaves on your face every time you go back to him
I don't have to be your type
I might even be unattractive to you
You could do better, if no one ever told you
I mean you keep falling for his crap and look how he's treating you
The sex must be good the way he's tricking you
Doesn't he have another girl?
Your man is playing you

Saying I'm too nice when he's misusing you
You're doing good for yourself
that's what he sees in you
A girl getting paid only so he could beg from you
Heart to heart
Friend to friend
I'll never see what you crave about your boyfriend
Hopefully he'll do better
I just can't see myself as your friend

How I Feel About You

Just as the predator watches its prey
I can't take my eyes off of you
Patiently waiting as an hourglass drops the last grain of sand,
only to be reset
This is how I think about you
I could piss off paparazzi and reporters with how much
I'm obsessed with you
Only if you knew
I never say much to you about it
This is how I feel about you

I Must Admit

I don't know how it started but
I must admit I'm glad it did
It's like a door opened that I wanted to stay closed
You're like the perfect mix of sins that I can't let go
Maybe it's your drive that makes me want you more
Whatever I'm feeling I can't let go!!!
Why I'm so into you?
It's like waking up in the morning and all I see is you
I'm brainwashed
All I think about is you
Whatever you're doing got me loving you
I think I'm losing it
I hope I'm not shocking you
You might think I'm your biggest fan
Well that might be true
I don't know how to feel but
I must admit
I think I want you
Sorry for the mix feelings but
Damn just look at you

If You Asked

Sometimes I just sit thinking about you
Asking Christ "could she be what I prayed for?"
It just feels so weird to me
Like everything I ever wanted is before me
Crazy to say, but I believe Christ is testing me
Bringing you in my life because it's good for me
I'll never know what you see when you look at me
It just feels weird because you bring out the best in me
Why do I feel this way?
You're like the perfect dream I don't want to go away
And every time I look around I see your face
How can we be friends when I feel another way?
Not saying it's not possible but my emotions keep getting in the way
All because everything I asked for is in my face
And if we shall ever separate I'll still feel the same
I'll never know how you feel when you're around me
"If you asked"
But I'm afraid to awake from this dream
Whatever we share means a lot to me
I'll never know why you chose me
"If you asked"
No, don't wake me from this dream

I'm Too Late

It amazes me how I never tried
You were the perfect image of my best desires
Everything a man wanted, but now my time expired
How could I not seen the signs?
You were basically throwing it at me
Now you can't be mine
You know I sometimes wonder how
we would've been together
Only if I could turn back the hands of time
I can't
Why can't I?
Maybe because you're taken now and very loyal
Damn how time flies
You have a kid now
I'm just out here in the world dreaming that
it could've been our child
Life goes on I guess, right?
Well
I guess there's no need to think about our future now, right?
I'll just sit here and wonder why I didn't try
You know each girl that told me that they would've gave me a chance
really opened my eyes

Damn! Just to hear "I wish you would've said something" really messes me up every time
To know that you were actually waiting for me to ask you out
I never did like rejections
Like it's one thing to get turn down by girls
that look decent
But getting turned down by girls
that's overly beautiful hurts even more
Why didn't I ever say anything?
Well
It's too late now

Nice Girl

I look at you and lost I become
In your eyes
In your smile
In your personality
We talked sometimes
Met up from time to time
Seeing each often as we pass some time
I'm not yours and you're not mines
Let's just share the moment and flow with the grind
I looked in your eyes and lost I became
In your flaws
In your smell
In the way you run your fingers through your hair
You don't complain
You're not loud
You stay to yourself
You're always proud
We built a friendship
That I never felt before
Now here we are living for what's in storage

Only Time Will Tell

I value our friendship more than you know
I cherish our bond more than you know
I wanted to say how I really feel
You already know
It's crazy how we love each other
We never said so
Maybe not in the same ways
We know so
I guess I am a little too straight forward
At least you know
I'll do anything for you
Only if you say so
There is one thing that you should know
I'll love you forever, even if you let go
Just let me know how far you're willing to go
No need for rushing, beautiful
We can take things slow
Just letting you know that I'm not letting you go
I'm going to love down on you
Until you can't take no more
What makes me love you so much is how you love me
Not speaking of a relationship
Not even about sex
You support me so much
Your care is best

Let's not worry about what's to come
What will happen next
Our friendship is good enough
Our support for each other is best
I cherish us more than you believe
Only time will tell, right?
Just promise me one thing
That you won't give up on me
Maybe I lied
Promise me that we'll always be friends, beautiful
If we're meant to be
Well only time will tell, right?

Scared

I never felt this way before
I'm so into you
Words can't explain how much I want you
How much I like you
You're just so beautiful and everything just so natural
I don't know what to make of it
I love you
Everything about you deserves to be loved
I honestly think of you as a gift from God
You're just so…
It's hard for me to explain
Just one smile from you brighten up my day
It's like I'm saying hello when my heart is saying bae
You're everything I ever wanted in a woman
There's more I want to say
You know how I only talk about school
and having a good career someday
Well I pictured you in my future
but with a ring and a baby on the way
Maybe I'm just too late
Afraid to step to the plate
You're just all I want despite our different ways
I want to love you unconditionally
and make you my wife
This is more than just words to me
I want you in my life

I don't care if we never make that extra step
Just don't leave my side
It's crazy how you get the best of me
Friends and all but you're that girl for me
I can never picture another girl
since you locked eyes with me
Too good of a conversation you know
Talking about our goals after we earn our degrees
Please don't let this just be words
You mean so much to me
Both of us focusing on school right now
That's cool with me
Both of us not ready for a relationship right now
Sound like a good plan to me
I just don't want to be scared no more
You know having to deal with you rejecting me
Might sound childish
I never felt this way before
I always feared the possibilities
Now I'm taking a chance
So I need to know,
Do you like me?

Speechless

For once in my life I met a woman
I can connect with
Coming from a professional and personal place
I met this woman and
She was somebody just like you
A Christian woman and
A scholar too
I met this woman and she was beautiful
Inside and out
She reminds me of you
For once in my life
I felt loved
Touched by an Angel
With God's blessings from above
I met this woman who taught me to be a friend
To lean not into my own understanding but
To follow Christ plan
For once in my life I met a woman I wouldn't mind being with
Just the way she makes me feel inside
I get that same feeling when
I look into your eyes
I met a woman
That I don't want to lose
She was an Angel just like you
Maybe I'm daydreaming because
She is you
Got me feeling speechless but
I dedicated this poem to you

Trust Issues

You didn't have to lie to me
You could've just been honest
Worrying about my feelings
going to leave you wondering
Let's just be honest
Have you ever noticed how I never get mad?
Keep your mind pondering on that bull crap
I put in your head, right?
Funny how you can take my sensitivity for weakness
Thinking I'm lost in the head, right?
You trying to utilize your womanly possessions
Even your pretty eyes and hourglass behind not going to make up for
the liar that lies inside of you
Thinking you weren't like the others
Maybe this could've been something new
You're just like these other girls
I can't trust you

We Can't Be Friends

As hard as I try to consider you as just a friend
I just can't
I just won't
Like who am I fooling, you mean more to me
I mean I can act like you don't
I'd be lying to myself
You told me not to lie to you right?
Well I want you
You just can't see me in that way though, right?
Yeah being in a relationship beyond our friendship
could mess up what we have
Whatever the hell that is
I just can't see you as being just a friend
We shared so much
Like me helping you get over your man
That was to make room for me
Not for you to go and end up in another man's arms
It's crazy
We even talked about me wanting to step up
but I'm not hood enough right?
I don't call you out your name and cheat on you right?
Hold up
Wait one damn minute
Is it because I'm not hard enough?
You don't want no soft guy, right?
Someone who'll treat and respect you

like the queen that you are
Maybe if I just told you that I just wanted to have sex and leave
I could've had a chance, right?
Maybe I should've just asked for sex and got up and walked off
I'm not like them other guys that said they loved you
I'm not even mad though
Just expressing how much I care about you
I would say that I love you too
It's love that's hurting you
I'm sorry
We can't be friends if we can't be friends and more
This is not by force
You could take your time
Just know
You could live your life being lied to and literally screwed all the time
You could consider my offer and let me show you what real love is
Just saying

NOTES

NOTES

PROJECTS

Brick By Brick

I once been marked from living in the projects
Been given certain looks for telling others that I was born and raised
in the projects
Why people look down on the projects?
Just another way of living to me
We can't even do that
As a matter of fact
Why people from the projects have to be considered "them people"
That's being judgmental
If even that
Not everyone that live in the projects are thugs
or gang bangers
Not everyone are drug users or drug dealers either
I just might be blind
I see greatness in the projects
Beautiful things come out of the projects
Instead of talking down on us
how about you help uplift us
So many people talking nonsense
but never step one foot in the projects
People throwing stones at us

Won't use them same stones to help rebuild the projects

Maybe it's just me but I love where I'm from

Yes, things weren't always great

I miss where I'm from

I honestly wish that I was rich

So I can rebuild where I'm from

Starting brick by brick

I'm from Chicago's projects

My very first home

Concrete

What am I to do now?
Born into a blessed Christian household
that doesn't exist now
Good memories of living in the projects
exist in my soul now
Mother told me these your Godmothers
Both are deceased now
Reminiscing the late 90s into the 2000s
How much I've grew now
Mixed cement of the past cracked into my future
as I walked alone
Trying to reach higher grounds
Where I'm to go now?
The sun faded leading into the night
The cold breeze of Autumn unites with my flesh
Shaking my spirit into being pissed
As I spit fling of rejection
only if I could've seen my own reaction of frozen mucus
I walk the slippery slopes that's cracking my path
Black ice in October
What's the point of the forecast
Cement from the bricks where I use to reside
Leaving nothing but dust and rocks
which opened my eyes
I'll never walk on the same concrete again
Since the projects died

Heartless

Was it worth it?
You taking another life so you worth it
Fake gang bangers
Y'all don't know what it means to ride or die
Putting murder cases on the boldest ones
Letting these minors hold y'all guns
Now their lives are destroyed
Crazy how they thought they was getting money
toward their bail
Y'all won't even write them a letter
Their families crying
Deep inside they're in that jail cell dying
Thinking to themselves "only if I didn't want to be cool"
These kids are growing up looking up to y'all
Thinking what y'all doing is worth idolizing
Now y'all get to sit back and let these kids do y'all dirt
It pisses me off how yet another kid gets shot
over y'all bullshit
Now that kid's face is y'all fashion statement
No pointing fingers but we all have to do better
It's sad how y'all so heartless
Was it worth it?
How do we allow this to happen?

Hood Life

How can I be a "thug" when I'm not hardcore?
How can I be a "gang banger" when I'm not in a gang?
What makes me a threat to you?
Why am I a target to you?
What did I do to you?
NOTHING!
What are you doing to me?
Racial profiling!
You may look at me and see that I'm dark skin
Walking along minding my own business
How am I a threat to you?
Awe yeah I remember
Not only are you afraid that I'm dark skin
Hold up let me count the ways
I'm educated
Have a real job, plus a career
I never been to jail
Never sold drugs
Never shot anybody
Never been in a gang, as I told you before
Yet I'm a target because of my hood life
Because you want me to do wrong when I'm doing right
Hood or not, I'm not your target
Stop racial profiling
I'm living my life

In Remembrance Of

The street lights are on
Mother yelling my name
Rushing me to say goodnight
Them street lights are on
Looking for something to eat
Pot luck would be nice
Finding myself sitting on the sofa with my mother
Cherishing a bowl of Lucky Charms
I wonder why the Leprechaun
never came back to the hood
Watching Sanford and Son while waiting on the Jefferson's, or
Good Times to come on
Crazy how even in hard times
there were hard times TV shows for Black people
Trying to still believe in that silver lining
Devotion turns into emotions, as I reminisce on how
The struggle kissed my siblings and I
I once played beside the worse kids
since I didn't have many friends
Pretending made my true colors disappear
Never understood much
Just knowing beautiful things came out of the projects
Only if I could go back
Back to the days when living in the projects

Were just daily celebrations

Messed me up every time

Trying to look toward the hills

While seeing yet another pair of sneakers

Hanging from the power lines

Bittersweet salt and sour, of the blessings and memories as my pen reminisces

In the remembrance of the projects

You will always be my first home

In These Streets

I see you
You're doing what's right
You're living your life
Blood in and blood out, right?
Well what about the next life?
What about me?
What about your babies?
Well I guess they're older now
I looked up to you
I followed behind you
I wanted to be something like you
Now look at you
Now look at me
Trying to be something that I can't be
Trying to do things that's not in me
All for respect, right?
Well I guess I'm just too soft, right?
There's no thug in me, right?
I'm not that hard, right?
Yet I once was you, trying to live the street life
I'm nothing like you
You're nothing like me

Something about children getting killed
Changed the best in you and me
We're changing lives
Beat the odds
Let's stay away from being a number
Taking our streets back is where we won
It was all in my head, right?

NOTES

NOTES

OPEN CONFESSIONS

I Could've Been More Honest

I could've told you that I had feelings for you

I should've just said that I had intentions

It was never you to be honest

Yeah you look decent as ever, since I'm being honest

It just wasn't ever you

I saw how much I was willing to give up

I never saw you for who you are as a person

Let's just be honest

I wanted you as much as I hated to admit it

Finding out that you were actually bisexual and I didn't

Want to be a part of that

I never was willing to say how much I wanted you

Not to have sex, but to be a part of you

Never was I sure of what I wanted but

I know that I was into you

I can't picture myself having a relationship

With the same sex

Even if I did try to have sex, it wouldn't work out

You were actually willing to go all the way

You literally knew what you wanted

While I was stuck on child's play

I can't see myself going with the same sex but

Always asking to hang out

You could get ANY girl you want but choose not to

Let's just be honest

Like dude you're very handsome

And EVERY girl wants you
I never understood guys being Bisexual but I'm not
Knocking it either
I once said that I was Bi too because I thought it was for
Whichever boy or girl stopped by
I thought about coming over but I knew you wouldn't
Come over either
I could've been more honest but you weren't honest Either
There was nothing between us but unsaid feelings and a
Spare of the moment to have oral sex
Honestly, I'm glad I got this off my chest because girls Surround you
I'm trying to be where the girls at

I Should Tell You

I should tell you
I should tell you
I should
Tell
But how do I start?
How to begin?
It feels like I had just as much of the blame
How would you feel?
Should I be ashamed?
Am I to blame?
I can't shake these memories off my mind
I'll never be the same
How to live life now?
I was a child
Just starting to understand things
I wish someone would've paid more attention
Now there are things I can't undo
Some "games" led to the wrong things
Knowing the difference from wrong and right but
I didn't learn everything
Christ put it in my heart to come clean so
I've played "fun games"
Not knowing at the time that it was all gay things
Thinking in my mind that we have the same things
Who's bigger?
Longer?
Have more hair and looks better?

Touch mines and I'll touch yours
Let's see whose rock is fatter
Grinding flesh because
It felt better
How do it taste?
I saw this on a flick
Let's see who could get it wetter
It's crazy
We were just kids
If getting bullied wasn't enough
Even your "school friends" had some things to show you
So called "cool people" got the best of me
Not fully understanding what was happening but
It was hurting me
Finally learned of my actions and
Broke the biggest sin in the Bible
It's sad to admit that was my first introduction to sex
Two boys aren't supposed to be that cool with each other but
That's what I was use to
Sad to say but
I still continued with other boys as far as oral
Never knew that after all these years
Still giving and taking oral is one hell of a drug
Crazy to say that
Believe it or not but
I'm still a virgin
Fighting daily not to have sex with the first girl that offer herself to me
I still believe in sex after marriage
Which makes me a target to most sexual women

I just had to come clean to myself

Most of all before Christ who delivered me

Let not your life be destroy by things you done or happened to you

For I am free now

Free from my past

Free from the enemy

This is what I should've told you

This is what I just told you

PS: TAKE TIME OUT TO TALK WITH PEOPLE THAT YOU LOVE (YOUNG AND OLD), AND YOUNG MEN AND WOMEN PLEASE DON'T BE AFRAID TO TALK TO SOMEONE THAT YOU TRUST, NO MATTER WHAT IT IS, THERE IS HELP OUT HERE FOR YOU.

I Wish I Would

Now that my phase of trying to be something that I'm not is over
I can speak the truth now
Allow me to start off by saying what in the world I was thinking?
Only a few of you was actually worth it
Was it worth it?
Me breaking the rules just to feel something real
It feels like it wasn't real
Me giving into temptation
I wouldn't say you all were 'all that'
But I needed to let go of some stress
I told you that our habits wasn't going to last
It was fun while it lasted but you wanted too much
Sorry for the words but what the hell is wrong with you?
Maybe it was me because I became your addiction
As you became mines
No holding back here
What we done needed some attention
I know for sure that I'm not perfect but it's wrong
Sorry if I led you on but what we was doing is wrong
Get over it
Life will go on
I'm down for still being cool
But nothing will be going on
I made a promise to Christ

And yes, I still have my virginity
I never penetrated nothing
You the one that opened your mouth to me
Well I did the same
I already said too much though
Welcome to my new identity
I wish I would go down that path again
I'm done

I'm Not A Faggot

Yes, I'll admit it
It hurts
They say words shouldn't affect you
Well sh...
I'm hurt
Before I even knew what a faggot was
And meant, it just hurt
I never deserved it
Being treated and looked upon as an outcast
Right before you got to know me
You seen that I wasn't nothing like you
Never tried to fit in
You didn't want to get to know me
Just separated yourself while trying to put a label on me
Stop trying to put the blame on me
I was born to be different and stand out
You barely even know me
And want to disrespect my name now
So I'm a disgrace and disappointment that you are
Ashamed of now
All because I'm different, with different interests
I got to be called a faggot now
Yeah that sh... hurts me
I love females but most of them don't love me back
Friend zone after friend zone

Knowing few were tempting to me

Gone through a phase knowing that wasn't like me

Why females don't like me?

Well keep calling me a faggot is not helping me

I guess your intentions was to really hurt me

I might be a little sensitive but there's no faggot in me

No disrespect or shade

I just had to show the real me

Let It Go

Yeah, I done some things, I'll admit that

No need to talk down at me when EVERYBODY done some messed up things

I'm man enough to own up to my downfalls and sins

No need to mention names

Because that wouldn't do any good

I prayed to the Heavens because

What wasn't said was already understood

I put my head down in shame while asking for forgiveness

To remove ALL my sins and keep them in the past

I'm stepping over ALL my bad habits

And what I use to have

It's a brand-new day and I'm loving what Christ allows me to have

What Christ allows me to do and become in life

I will NEVER consider myself to be better or worse than others

I too fall short of Christ mercy and grace just like any Other human being

Life will happen to the point

That flashbacks start to flash forward

I'm stronger than before

Knowing of my acts and knowing that my actions opens and closes doors

My sins and bad habits STILL knocking on my door

Party over here but I have so much to live for

People STILL testing me but my past is no more

My feet hurt from standing for what I believe in

Yeah, some things are VERY tempting
But that is the old me
Something like them times I smoked weed
I tried it a few times and smelled a sinner on me
I had a few shots and felt a sinner nearly control me
I looked at girls in sexual ways
Neither of us had rings on our fingers
I guess that's why my hormones keep raging everyday
I spoke to Jesus and he told me to pray
To keep praying and pray when I already prayed
So I prayed some more and all my sins went away
Jesus told me to let it go

NO Regrets

I look in your eyes and yet it feels like Deja-vu
Getting lost in the stories that I've been through
Feels like no one cares
You could just go your own way
Once the fun is over will you
Feel good about yourself the next day?
I must say of course it wasn't planned
You've finally enjoyed yourself
And things got out of hands
You knew what you were getting yourself into
You took that chance
Took a big risk
Got caught up in the moment faster than a first kiss
That dismiss
Leaving that person's house feeling better but shameful
Thinking to yourself
"is it alright to admit that I liked it?"
Whatever happened is done now
Just be bold enough to admit it if anything goes down
Don't dwell on what happened
What could've happened
What you wanted to happen
Just let it be a lesson learned
No regrets as the pages turn

The Moment I Realized

I once was asked if I was gay
No, I lied
I'm continuously asked if I am gay
Judged from the way that I acted
To the way I carried myself
Judged from the way I allowed myself to speak soft
Misunderstood, so you said that I was soft
Spoke the words into my head
Had me believing that I was soft
Had me believing that I was gay
Some would still ask me
Why I feel this way?
Words are powerful so
You tell me why you spoke gayness into my life?
I was not born gay you know
I've been called a faggot so much
I started to believe it was ok
Well it's not!
I was a fucking child and you all spoke that bullshit
My way
"Stop acting soft"
"You are acting like a faggot"
"You are a faggot"
"Man the fuck up"
Not every boy wants to man up
When they are still a child

I will never understand what it meant to have a Childhood
Why?
Because of people like you
I was afraid, you know
Bullies came my way, you know
I was not going to say anything but
Most of them was on the downlow
It took me 21 damn years to realize that I am not gay
To realize that I'll never speak words that can impact
Somebody's life in the wrong way
The moment I realize that the power of life and death
Lies within the tongue
I started to speak life
The moment Christ told me to speak things
Into existence
I spoke homosexuality out my life
It was that very moment when I realized
I was living what you spoke into me
So I changed my reality
I am still without a girlfriend
It is a start for me

Too Many Women

Only if I didn't feed into people nonsense
Only if I could undo somethings
Never really understood what a gay person was
What a bisexual person was
Even what a straight person was
I mean due to personal beliefs,
I honestly wasn't raised to discriminate
To think about it
All the times I been called gay or a faggot
Nobody should be judging me
You know how people always saying
"be careful what you say to kids"
Well that saying is true
I must say if it wasn't for Jesus Christ delivering me and
Giving me the strength to talk about it now
I just wish somebody would've paid more attention
Before it all started
The good thing about life is that we all have choices and able to learn
from them
I'm what you call Poetry
That is how I choose to define myself
To be a feeling or an emotion that could connect with
Anyone or anything

Now that I'm older and I know who I want to be

I honestly feel that it's too many women in the world to

Be out here chasing man parts

I can't be disrespectful

I'm cool with people that love them man parts

Only a few will understand, but I love my queens

NOTES

NOTES

SAVED IN CHRIST

Amen

I spoke your name
Talking to you in prayer
I walked with you
Knowing you'll take me there
To that special place where I can find peace
Where I can feel joy
Feeling your presence in my spirit
I call on your name some more
Hosanna! Hosanna! Hosanna!
For I changed my life
You been with me all along
The blood you shared
The way you died
Sacrificing your life so
You could save mine
You returned with power
All power in your hands
I surrender all
My life now belongs to you
After all is done
After everything is in your hands
There's one word I can say
that word is, Amen

Anointed

From the time I was a child
I played church
Preaching the word of God
Since I went to church
Trying to sound like the preacher I heard that day
It's just something about the way I was able to use
my own words
It was something about the way I just played
Actually being a believer of Christ but
It's just something about the way I played
I received the best rest sleeping in the choir stand
While the preacher was preaching
Sleeping in the church
You know all the way in the back row of the sanctuary
Crazy how I sometimes can still recall what was said
I fully submitted my life to Christ at a young age
Taking the roll as a singer and praising Jesus name
Without knowing I became a servant
A part of the body of Christ
Overly happy to be a part of Christianity
I was trying to find the anointed but
It's already in me
Yes I'm anointed
Jesus touched me when he blessed me to be born
Wow! It was me
Anointed since birth

Come By Here

(A gospel song into poetry)

The homeless need you Lord
Come by here
People getting sick Lord
Come by here
The crime rate going up Lord
Come by here
O Lord come by here
And as elders once said "Kumbaya" (Ku ba Yah)
For there's a praying grandmother somewhere Lord
Kumbaya
Young men and women going to jail Lord
Kumbaya
Diseases after diseases Lord
Kumbaya
O Lord, Kumbaya
Young ladies, at young ages, having babies Lord
Kumbaya
Guns and drugs, I'm praying it ends Lord
Kumbaya
O Lord, Kumbaya

Eli Sankofa

I was sitting down thinking
Thinking about my life
The television set was speaking to me
Had a cool nickname in high school
I didn't know what it meant
Planning to not plan, once got out of hand
Saying I like myself when
The love was pretend
I knew I was born but
Was it to win?
Blessings after blessings but
Don't forget about the sins
People walked away for not understanding
It's my life I'm living and I still don't understand it
Worked my way up just to be noticed
I lead as a Christian but
Sometimes I lose focus
I was told to keep learning and I'll find my purpose
History is my drive but
I wouldn't say I know everything
Writing is my life but
I could be doing better things
Christ is my all
That's why I live life
Given the platform to teach
I am ascended by Christ to go back
Eli Sankofa

For My Miracle

I'm alive

I'm alive

No time to look back

I'm not talking back

I'm alive

I'm alive

I took the risk

I made the living

Walked on the same grounds as the forgotten

I'm alive

I'm alive

I thank Christ

Who saved my life?

I fell from humbleness

I lost for trying

I'm alive

I'm alive

I ran from the unheard

I hid from the unspoken

I can't be found

Whose lives have been taken?

I made the choices

I took the blame

I changed your life

Now you're not the same

I asked for forgiveness

Both Heaven and Earth

I'm alive

I'm alive

It's a miracle

I've been delivered

I've been healed

I've been changed

I'm not the same

Oh I thank you Lord, for my miracle

For Your Glory

I'll dance like David if I have to
Pray like a grandmother if I have to
Sing to the heavens above, if I have to
Cry out for your grace and mercy if I have to
For your glory

From The Hills

I imagine myself standing on the hill where your love
Showed for me
Teardrops like snowflakes, turning into the ice age
Healing from the hell that we're living through each day
Standing on the hill just thinking of the blood running
Down your face
Carrying your own death
While them devils hammer away
Yelling from the hill where history was made
I just pray that all your pain didn't go to waste
Humans killing humans, despite their race
Raping and cheating is a slap in your face
Taking your own life would put you in the wrong place
There's Ten Commandments and most of them we break
66 books and we only pick them up when it's too late
Standing on the hill, wondering what would've happened if
Jesus didn't complete the 7th day
From the hills I yell loud to
only imagine myself standing right beside him

God Will

God will make a way
Might be out of my mind
There were so many times
I felt like I wasn't supposed to be alive
God will bring you out
When I was going through my trials and tribulations
Something about the name Jesus just ease my burdens
So I could walk out
For I know that God will make a way
I've seen it and he will, when I'll cry out my pain
God will take the pain away
When people would switch up and change
God will be there for me through sunshine and rain
For God will make a way
I know that he will
I've seen it and he will
Only if you let him make a way

Heaven Or Hell

I sit at the table with two pens in my hands
One in the left and the other in the right
Two contracts
One on my left and the other on my right
Here I am sitting at the table of life
Had the chance to taste a bite of both
Now my name must go on a black line
Sad to say but it's been passed my signing day
Two pens in my hands
No speeches, I learned both of their ways
As I reside in the middle
A place called Earth
Heaven and Hell is what I see when I step out my door
No introduction
Breaking news, wondering what I'm waiting for?
Broke out in a cold sweat from sitting
In the middle of good and evil
For what is good could be evil and
What is evil could feel great
I'm still alive
No judgement day
Two different books
Just waiting on my due date
I once walked the path of gray areas

No staying there, I'm feeling better
The time I shared in the middle forced me to take a stand
Christ is where I belong!
Signed the contract on my right and told the
Devil to get the hell on
Welcome to a new beginning

I Say Yes Lord

I'm done fighting

That wasn't my style anyway

Let people get inside my head

Not taking back what I said

For it happened already

Lord knows how I feel

I can't keep hiding behind my fears

Lord I say yes to your will and your way

For you're the only one who can take the pain away

I'm Being Watched

In my wrong
You're watching me
When I'm doing right
You're watching me
You wrote the story
Made the plans
Said go here to there
Now here I am
In your mercy, In your glory
You told me to live
Now I'm telling my story
I've done wrong
I've done good things too
You told me to stand still
Now I can move, Move right on
I'm being watched
The story continues on

I'm Changing

I've left the old me behind and starting on the new me

This is not a dream

I'm living with nothing but all victories within me

My past, that's history

Not me but his story

The old me that lived through it

It's a brighter day

The beginning of a fresh start and a new mindset

What can I say I'm changing

From the day I realized I don't have many friends and everything felt like it's pretended

I begin to pretend like everything

Was like a walk in the park

Until you messed with the right one and had to find out

That I do have heart

I'm changing and all for the right ways and reasons

Not trying to be the one that gets locked up

I'm playing or I'm teasing?

My emotions are like the forecast in Chicago

You can't predict the weather and seasons

I'm changing just like the seasons

Trying to get me some lifetime friends and leave these

Seasonal clowns alone

I'm changing, for I am who I am
I am an overcomer and leader
Positive with motivation in my life
I'm changing, for I'm a winner
Great person and blessed
There's no need to look at my past
When Jesus is in my life and future
For I've changed with a bright and promising future

I'm Not The Only One

I'm finding myself

I'm coming into my own

Felt like I was walking by myself

Jesus been here all along

Through my sins and my prayers

Through the wrongs and the spells

Felt like no one cared, so I did what I've done

I've been told to walk with Jesus

He sees all and knows all, so I couldn't run

Sinning after sinning

I wasn't the only one

Yeah, I'm finding myself

Blessed to be coming into my own

So yes, I'll stand with Jesus

I believe in no regrets

Only moving on

Jesus Christ

Jesus!!! Jesus!!! Jesus!!!

Oh how you save me

Oh how you healed me

Oh how you delivered me

I can't stop thinking about you

I just don't want to be without you

You always been by my side

You NEVER let me go

Oh Jesus!!!

You are so good to me

Even in my wrong, you still bless me

I could've been dead multiple times

But Jesus!!! Jesus!!! Jesus!!!

Oh Jesus!!!

You didn't have to do it, but you did Lord

Now I understand what the elders been talking about Lord

I can't make it without you Lord

Jesus!!! Jesus!!! Jesus!!!

Oh Jesus!!!

I'm nothing without you Lord

Nobody like you Lord

Thanks for showing me the way Lord

I love you Lord!!!

My Lord and Savior Jesus Christ

Lost

Sometimes I just stare in the mirror wondering
What do I see
Obviously it's a reflection of me but
Who's that person staring back at me?
Face to face, he locked eyes with me
Moving at the same pace as me
I'm not about to blink
He probably doesn't blink with me
Seems crazy but who's this dude looking at me?
I'm looking in the mirror but I don't like what I see
Saying to myself my name is Lavell Harris as I
Think about what that use to mean
What I use to see
Changing my image and name temporary because
I didn't like how Lavell Harris carried me
Why is my past looking back at me?
Trying to remind me of what I used to be
What I use to be is now showing me the new me
See the Devil tried to keep me in my past, while…
Jesus is showing me my reality
Knowing it's not about who I was or was becoming
But who I want to be and what Jesus
Is allowing for me
So now I can see why the reflection was staring at me
Not because it's a reflection but because it saw what I Didn't see

Use to be lost but Jesus found me
Use to be blind but Lavell saved me
Opened my eyes and made me see
Hi I'm Lavell Harris
I love myself, I love myself deeply

My Due Season

I pray when it's time to pray
I pray when it's not time to pray
I thank Jesus Christ in my victories
I thank Jesus Christ for learning from my mistakes
I sometimes give more then I should've
Knowing I needed help too
Knowing I needed a prayer too
Some will ask me how I'm so blessed
While others wondering how I'm making it through
I sometimes look at myself
I sometimes look at you
Saying we don't look like what we been through
Jesus is good
I know he is
For it's not my doing
It's not my saying
But Jesus Christ gave us all powers
Our powers are praying
Speaking things into existence
Having faith
For my due season is coming
Yours on the way

My Prayer

My father who are in heaven

I come to you today in need of help

I am living in a world full of killing and diseases

Hatred and people being mistreated

I am praying for the broken homes

Children who feel alone

People going astray Oh Lord

It feels like there is no way-out Jesus

I am praying for a change my Lord

Some sign of deliverance my Lord

We need you Oh Lord

I need you Oh Lord to fix my mind when I am thinking poor

We are living life Jesus

Some of us do not know what for

I pray you lead us in the right direction

Cover us with your protection

For I come to you Oh Lord asking to just move in me like never before

Allow me to serve you and only you Oh Lord

Be my go to when I am doing wrong Oh Lord

I pray that you deliver the ones that may be struggling Jesus

Let them know that they do not have to fight no more

That we do not have to worry no more

That everything can go back the way it was Oh Lord

And I ask of this and so much more in your name… Jesus Christ

Amen Amen and Amen

No Weapons Shall Prosper

You could take my body

You won't take my soul

Harm my flesh but not my soul

I might be afraid

You might kill my body but not my soul

For I am covered in the blood of Jesus

Safe and secure in the blood of Jesus

I might be leaking blood but I'm saved in Jesus

You can hit me

Stab me

Even shoot me I'll still be alright in the blood of Jesus

Stone me to death if you like

While I'm being stoned I'll be thinking about Jesus

You know words hurt more than any weapon in this world

So I'll be calling on the name of Jesus through it all

Catch me struggling or catch me doing good in life

It doesn't matter how I'm living

I just want Jesus by my side

So do what you must do

Just know that no weapon formed against me shall prosper

Temptation

This is the day that I! turn my life over for the better

I've done wrong thinking that I! can make it on my own

I'm a sinner interacting in activities knowing that I'm a sinner

This is the day that I! choose to live right

The Devil keep calling me saying "I know you want to do right"

Your right is not Christ right trying to brainwash me so I won't do right

I! remember them nights

Calling myself speaking of Christ when the sins looked

good them nights

I knew it wasn't right

Somethings I'll never forget because it changed my life

This is the day that I! leave my past

Temptation got me on brick!

The things I use to think about man I was sicker than a you know what

Crazy how them videos actual are sins but changed my life

In the Bible it has that I should wait

Jesus Christ will reward me the soulmate that he wants me to have

Temptation still trying to attack me but I rebuke that sin every time in the name of Jesus!

For this is the day that I! will wait on Jesus Christ

Celibacy is a belief that I choose to obey

NOTHING wrong with waiting

I'm blessed to be a man never had sex

Temptation has its way but temptation also could lead to sin

I'll take my chances in Jesus Christ for I know I'll win

The Ways Of Sin

I've said some words that I shouldn't said
Made some decisions I could've talked about
Now I'm afraid and you're afraid
Afraid of what may happen
Afraid of what could be said next
And Lord! I apologize
I apologize from the depths of my soul!
Now I can't unsay what's been said
Now I can't undo what's been done
Now we're both afraid
Not you Lord! But the ones the Devil use me to get to
To speak at
It hurts my soul! To think about what I allowed to happen
How I allowed myself to be locked behind doors separated from the
rest of the world
To allow myself to say the things I said to my own
I'm in pieces! But I've learned
I've overcame
Now I conquer
The ways of sin

Young King

I look in the mirror and ask myself what do I see?

A boy, a man

Maybe just a human being

I ask myself how I feel?

How I should feel?

Something feels so fake but... making me feel real

What is real? And could real define me?

I feel so scared

Maybe it's my past behind me

Why must you define me?

I am who I am but you want to hide me

Place me away from the known and unknown

You had your fun now life must go on

Can I go on?

Living my life as this big lie

Wearing the mask of excitement when behind it I want to cry

Why must I die?

What's with the WHY?

Now I become a man just watch me rise

I nearly can fly no wings needed when these blunts got me high

When these shots got me by, I wasn't taking communion

It's not even Sunday yet and I'm ready to clap my hands

Stomp my feet praise the Lord for helping me find me!

To know and understand my self-worth

Thinking I'm just looking at my reflections when

I was looking at a young king

Christ created me to be a king

Now I shall walk

Walk into my victory

NOTES

NOTES

NOTES

NOTES

NOTES

PS: For more information or bookings, please email
h.lavell@yahoo.com

And
Please leave feedback and share

Thank You ☺

Do not forget to read

Book 1

"Flow: The Feeling Of A Poet"

Flow: The Feeling Of A Poet is a poetry short book that is based on daily life. Author Lavell Harris covers a host of daily issue and situation that he himself once encounter during his younger life, which sparked a flame inside of him to share his experiences on how he overcame the challenges in his life. Flow: The Feeling Of A Poet is not just a poetry book, but Lavell's journal of coping, which he shares real stories and inner emotions toward violence, low self-esteem, faith, love, hate, pain, and more as he continues to learn how to cope through his poetry.